ANCIENT ROME

A GUIDE TO THE GLORY
OF IMPERIAL ROME

JONATHAN STROUD

NEW YORK

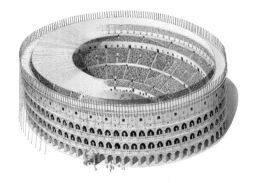

Written and edited by   Jonathan Stroud
Designer   Malcolm Parchment

Consultant   David Nightingale
Illustrations   Inklink Firenze
Kevin Maddison

KINGFISHER
Larousse Kingfisher Chambers Inc.
95 Madison Avenue
New York, New York 10016

First published in 2000
2 4 6 8 10 9 7 5 3 1

1TR/1199/WKT/AT(AT)/140MA

LIBRARY OF CONGRESS CATALOGING-IN-PUBLICATION DATA
Stroud, Jonathan.
Ancient Rome/by Jonathan Stroud.—1st ed.
p.   cm.—(Sightseers)
Includes index.
Summary: Looks at what life was like in ancient Rome, in a travel guide format.
ISBN 0-7534-5235-9 (hb)
1. Rome—Social life and customs—Juvenile literature. 2. City and town
life—Rome—Juvenile literature. 3. Rome (Italy)—Antiquities,
Roman—Guidebooks—Juvenile literature. [1. Rome—Social life and customs.] I. Title. II.
Series.
DG63 .S68 2000
937—dc21
99-040367

Printed in Hong Kong

Contents

Introducing Rome

Welcome to Rome, the greatest city in the world. It is the heart of the largest empire ever seen, ruling over millions of people in places as far apart as England and Egypt. Above all, it is a city of extremes. Filled with spacious palaces and public buildings, it is also the most crowded place on earth. One million people live here, crammed into the narrow streets. And although the empire's riches pour into Rome, over 200,000 people are unemployed and rely on the emperor for free grain.

The emperor Hadrian is rarely in Rome itself. He spends years traveling through the empire, protecting its frontiers and exploring many local cultures. However, he has still found time to organize new building projects in the capital.

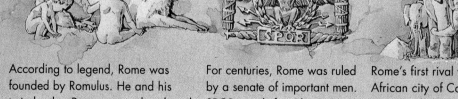

According to legend, Rome was founded by Romulus. He and his twin brother Remus were abandoned as babies, and raised by a wolf.

For centuries, Rome was ruled by a senate of important men. SPQR stands for *"the Senate and the People of Rome."*

Rome's first rival was the African city of Carthage. Its army used elephants to attack Italy, but was defeated.

Rome's weather is good, and people spend most of the time outdoors.

 In the Forum, look for the Rostra platform where political speeches are made.

 Rome has grown beyond its walls. Its empire is so strong, it needs no defense.

Rome's spiritual heart is the ancient Forum, or market place. Centuries ago, when Rome was a village, its people met in this open space to trade and discuss politics. Now the old square is built up with giant temples and political memorials, and the markets have moved elsewhere. The old ruling Senate House is still by the Forum, but Rome's real center of power is now the nearby emperor's palace.

Sightseers' tip
You will see vast differences in wealth here in Rome. A tiny elite is staggeringly rich, but one third of its people are slaves.

For 250 years after beating Carthage, Rome's efficient armies conquered all the lands around the Mediterranean Sea.

A great general, Julius Caesar, destroyed the Senate's power and ruled Rome alone, but he was murdered by the senators.

After Caesar's death, his adopted son Augustus took control. He became the first in a long line of emperors.

Traveling around

You should have no problems getting to Rome. It is at the center of the finest road system ever built. There are over 30,000 miles of superb highway covering the empire, all built by the Roman army. Communications are easier now than at any time in history, and you could cross the empire on horseback in just 100 days. Once you're in Rome itself, however, it's not always easy finding your way around. None of the thousands of winding streets have names or numbers.

If you can hitch a ride on a merchant ship, a great way to get to Rome is up the Tiber River. Hundreds of small craft sail to and from the coast, bringing grain, wine, and other supplies that the city needs.

A new road has very hard-wearing foundations. A flat layer of sand goes on the bottom, with layers of stone and gravel above. The road is topped with paving stones, which are domed to let rain run off. Road engineers use tools to keep their course as straight as possible, so that all distances are minimized.

On the way to Rome, keep an eye out for the milestones that tell you how far you have to go.

 If you get lost in the city, use temples and statues as landmarks to find your way.

 Take a slave with you if you go out at night. Thieves and muggers are common in Rome.

Sightseers' tip
If you can't find a bathroom, look for a urine jar. The contents of these are sold to cloth makers, who use it to dissolve fat and grease left in fresh wool.

Although rich people might travel around by sedan chair, by far the best way to get around Rome is on foot. There are raised sidewalks to keep you out of the mud and sewage on the streets, and stepping stones to help you cross. Walking also helps you to keep moving on the main streets, which stay busy even at night. Traders with noisy, slow-moving carts are only allowed into the city at dusk, and quickly block the streets. Traffic jams are common, as are lost tempers.

What to wear

Appearance is very important to the Romans, so you should try to fit in with their current styles. For instance, men have traditionally been clean-shaven, but the emperor has just started a fashion for wearing beards. Old-style togas are still worn for important occasions, but for everyday wear, the simpler tunic is now preferred.

Rich women have personal slaves to shape their hair in elaborate styles. This can take all morning. Others wear wigs made from the hair of foreign slaves—blonde hair from German women is thought to be very exotic.

Romans have plenty of tools to help improve their looks. You can buy combs, hairpins, tweezers for plucking hairs, and special little spoons for scraping wax out of your ears.

You can buy stick-on leather patches to cover any unsightly spots or scars.

Men must wear togas when visiting the law courts or on official business.

Roman women often use crushed ants' egg paste to darken their eyebrows.

Both men and women wear jewelry, including brooches to hold their cloaks in place. Snake bracelets are popular, as are gold necklaces set with precious stones.

Sightseers' tip

For women, a pale face is a status symbol. Poor women have rough, red faces from working outside. Use creams that contain flour, chalk, and lead to whiten your skin.

A fashionable Roman woman takes great care with her clothes. She first puts on an ankle-length woollen undertunic, with a colorful embroidered dress, or *stola*, on top. This can be made of wool, cotton, or silk. She then places a beautiful jeweled girdle around her waist. Wealthy men wear long tunics. Poorer men and slaves have shorter tunics, which give them more freedom as they work.

9

Food and drink

What you eat in Rome will depend on one simple thing: money. If you're rich, you can taste an unending array of exotic delicacies—from stuffed dormice to ostrich and flamingo. If not, you'll share most people's diet of grain boiled into porridge and mixed with cheap foods like eggs and cheese. For most Romans, meat is a rare dish. However, most people drink wine mixed with water. It is considered vulgar to drink wine undiluted.

Roman kitchens contain many spices and herbs. Spicy sauces are put on everything to cover the taste of rotting old meat or fish. The favorite sauce is *liquamen*, strained from salted fish guts left out in the sun.

Ovens are banned in Rome's crowded apartments because of the risk of fire. So many people don't cook at all, but visit streetside taverns to buy good food such as soup, sausages, pies, fried fish, and fruit. Other favorites include thin, round pastries topped with olives, fish, and onions. Tasty snacks like this are perfect for a light lunch.

At some parties, dancing and music are provided while guests eat.

Rome is a day's journey from the sea, so fish here is not very fresh.

Need a cure for indigestion? Try raw cabbage soaked in vinegar.

Party hosts try to impress their guests with fine silver dishes. Salads and oysters are often served as entrees, followed by several courses of game birds, boar, venison, hare, ham, and fish. Dessert is usually honey cakes and fruit.

Sightseers' tip At some banquets, where a lot of food is served, a room is set aside as a *vomitorium* for those who eat too much too quickly. By making yourself throw up in there, you can get ready for the next few courses!

At most dinner parties, the guests lie on three couches around a table. They support themselves on the left elbow, and hold their food in the right hand. Knives and spoons are rarely used, so most foods are quite solid and not served too hot. The host's slaves serve everyone, but guests sometimes bring their own slaves along to help out.

Shopping

Rome is the most incredible shopping center on earth. Every day, ships and wagons arrive from all over the empire, carrying goods made in distant corners of the world. Traders from as far as India and China bring back luxurious silks and spices to delight the wealthy buyers here. But there are many affordable things to buy, too: whether you want shoes, pots, or clothes, you'll find exactly what you want in Rome.

Rome is the richest city in the empire, and luxury goods are plentiful here. This vase, carved out of blue and white glass, took months to make, and only the very rich can afford to buy it.

Most Roman stores are stands or rooms opening out onto the street. Here you can buy many exotic things: wool from Britain, silver from Spain, carpets from Turkey, and perfumes from Iran. But of all the things on sale, by far the most important are the huge amounts of grain that arrive daily from Africa. Rome is so big that Italian farmers can't supply enough wheat, so imports are essential for feeding the poor. In hard times, the emperor gives free handouts of grain to the needy.

The newest and most spectacular place to shop in Rome is Trajan's Market near the Forum. Made using the latest technology, it is an enormous semicircular shopping center carved out of the side of a hill, with 150 stores, offices, and a central open space where traders can set up their stands.

To find a tavern, look for green boughs hanging over the door.

 The same coins are used across the empire, from Britain to Asia Minor.

 The best mass-produced red pottery comes from France.

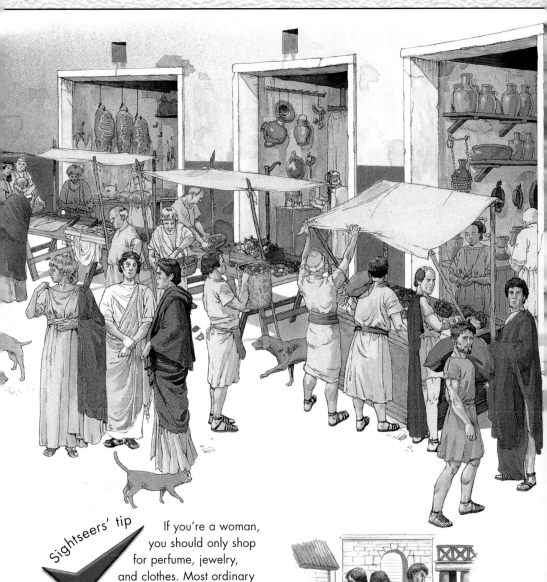

Sightseers' tip
If you're a woman, you should only shop for perfume, jewelry, and clothes. Most ordinary shopping is done by male slaves.

Slaves are brought to Rome from battlefields at the edges of the empire. You can pick them for their strength or looks, or for skills such as dancing, cooking, or music. Skilled slaves can cost 12 times as much as unskilled ones.

13

Accommodation

There are great differences in the quality of housing in Rome. The city sprawls over seven hills and all the richest people live in spacious villas on the airy higher ground. Everyone else crams into the ramshackle apartment houses that fill the valleys in between. In summer, these hot, overcrowded streets are a breeding ground for disease, and the few who can afford it leave the city for the country. Rich or poor, most people don't spend much time at home—they prefer to work and socialize outdoors, or in public places, such as the baths.

Sightseers' tip

Look out for the *vigiles*, Rome's seven squads of professional firemen. Each squad has 1,000 freedmen who tackle fires, and help keep order on the rowdy streets.

Unless you're very rich, you'll have to find a place to stay in one of the crowded tenement buildings that house most of Rome's population. It is a risky business— the stuffy apartments can catch fire easily, and are so badly made that they often fall down. Each building has up to six stories, with stores on the first floor. Ask for a room at the top—or the noise of traders' carts will keep you awake all night!

People with rooms to rent often paint "For Rent" on the side of the building.

Most houses are airy to keep you cool in summer. In winter, they can be freezing.

 The father is head of the family, but the mother runs the household.

A rich man's town house is built around the *atrium*, an open hall with a pool in the middle to catch water. Doors on both sides lead to the dining room, reception rooms, kitchen, and bedrooms. The atrium is the house's main source of light and air—outside walls have few windows, to keep out noise and burglars. At the back, a *peristyle*, or garden, filled with shrubs and statues, provides a tranquil spot for the family to escape the city's hubbub.

Even big houses don't have much furniture. The couches in the dining room are the most important items. By adding wool blankets, they double up as beds at night.

Many houses have small shrines where families worship their own personal gods, called *lares*. Every day, offerings of wine, cakes, and incense are made at the shrines, which contain tiny statues of the *lar*. If the offerings are made correctly, the lar will bring wealth and happiness to the household.

15

The baths

The public baths are an essential part of life in Rome. There are hundreds of baths in the city, and many people visit one every day to spend a few relaxing hours swimming, chatting, or playing games in magnificent surroundings. Most trips to the baths are free, because rich men pay everyone's fees in the hope of gaining votes or increasing their popularity.

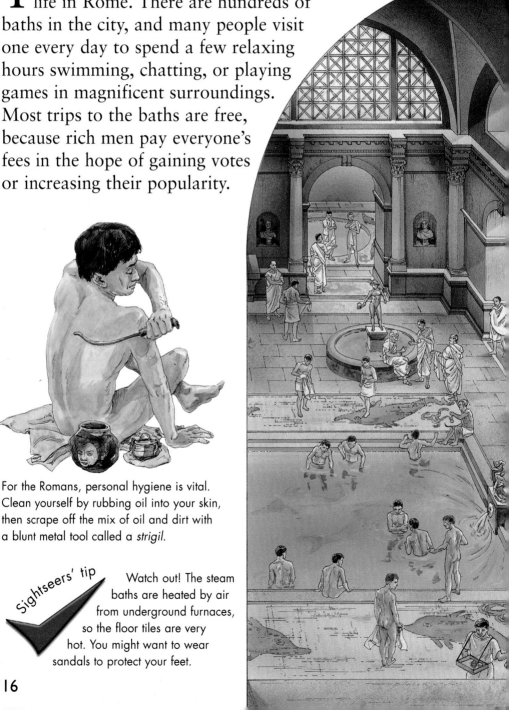

For the Romans, personal hygiene is vital. Clean yourself by rubbing oil into your skin, then scrape off the mix of oil and dirt with a blunt metal tool called a *strigil*.

Sightseers' tip

Watch out! The steam baths are heated by air from underground furnaces, so the floor tiles are very hot. You might want to wear sandals to protect your feet.

Hire a slave to guard your clothes—or they might get stolen.

Bathing times for men and women are indicated by a ringing bell.

Slaves sell tasty snacks to help you recover after a long swim.

All the baths are richly decorated. There are intricate mosaics on the floor, rooms are lined with marble pillars, and the ceilings are high and beautifully painted. All this luxury gives even poor people a regular taste of the power and wealth of Rome.

Don't miss the splendid public lavatories at the baths. Some can sit 16 people side by side, so you can talk with your friends comfortably. This is better than a toilet at home, which is usually just a pot in the corner.

There is a bewildering variety of rooms in the baths. They include hot and cold pools, steam rooms, saunas, and haircutting salons. The largest baths also have forecourts with stores, restaurants, and libraries. When you visit, warm up in the gymnasium by wrestling or playing ball games, then make for the *caldarium*—the hottest room of all—to bring yourself out in a cleansing sweat. After a good massage, finish with an invigorating dip in the ice-cold plunge pool.

17

The theater

Going to the theater is one of the Romans' favorite pastimes. There are several semicircular stone theaters in the city, hosting plays and games to celebrate recent victories. Shows last many hours, and there are several kinds to see. Although some Greek tragedies are performed, Romans prefer comedy, with a lot of crude jokes, fast action, and happy endings. Some characters are very popular, such as the cunning slave, who always manages to talk himself out of trouble in the nick of time.

Sightseers' tip Don't rent a room near a theater. To get good seats, a crowd will gather the night before a show—and they make a lot of noise. The emperor Caligula once ordered his guards to beat up a crowd after they kept him awake all night.

Free food and drinks are usually provided by the show's sponsor.

Theaters sometimes bring wild beasts on stage to attract larger crowds.

In some tragedies, a real-life criminal might be executed live on stage.

Actors rehearse in the building behind the stage. All the actors are men, but they play women's roles, too.

Romans love special effects—ghosts appear through holes in the stage floor and winches help produce gods from above. There is little scenery, although real chariots and horses sometimes appear on stage. Actors wear standardized masks, wigs, and colors to show what kind of character they are playing. If the crowd is pleased, they clap, snap their fingers and thumbs, and wave their togas—if not, they will hiss, shout, and make rude noises.

Music and songs accompany many plays. Greek instruments such as the stringed lyre or *cithara* are popular, as are the double pipes, cymbals, and tamborine, which can all be heard well in the open air.

The temples

Religion is an important part of life in Rome. Everything from personal health to success in war depends on the favor of the gods, and regular rituals must be carried out to keep them satisfied. In hundreds of temples across the city, special priests elected from among Rome's nobles perform sacrifices on behalf of the people. Festivals and feast days are held for each god, and offerings of fruit, wine, and animals are made every day.

Jupiter is the king of the gods, and Rome itself is under his protection. He also controls the sky and weather. Many other gods watch over other aspects of life. Some of the most important are Mars, the god of war; Apollo, the god of light and music; Vesta, the goddess of home and hearth; and Minerva, the goddess of wisdom.

Sightseers' tip

Want to know your destiny? The Romans are fond of divination—the interpretation of omens. Thunder, lightning, and the behavior of birds are studied and used to predict the future.

Sacred chickens are watched for omens during army campaigns.

During *Saturnalia*, the winter festival, people give each other presents.

Hadrian is said to have designed the Pantheon's dome himself.

Animal sacrifices are often carried out. Each animal must be a perfect physical specimen, and the more willingly it goes to the slaughter, the better the omen. Once dead, its entrails are studied: if they are in good condition, the body is cooked for the pleasure of the gods.

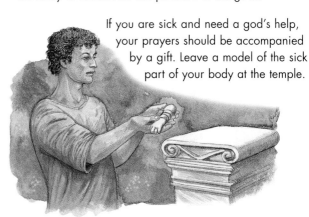

If you are sick and need a god's help, your prayers should be accompanied by a gift. Leave a model of the sick part of your body at the temple.

The newest, and one of the greatest, sights in Rome is Hadrian's Pantheon, a temple to all the gods. It is a masterpiece of engineering, with the world's widest dome (143 ft.), made from concrete poured over a temporary wooden framework. Statues of the gods line the walls. A single hole at the top, the *oculus*, provides the only light and represents the sun in the heavens.

21

Circus Maximus

If there's one unmissable sight in Rome, it's the Circus Maximus. This giant chariot-racing circuit is over 500 years old, and is by far the biggest stadium in the world. Up to 250,000 people can crowd in to watch the races—that's a quarter of Rome's population! Everyone comes here to cheer on their teams and gasp at the high-speed crashes. Entry is free to watch all of the day's 24 races.

Gamblers out there—beware! You can bet on chariot races and gladiator fights, but it is illegal at other times. Still, Romans love gambling, and many go to secret betting houses, where they can wager money on dice or on the tossing of coins.

Sightseers' tip
Keep an eye out for cheating. Drivers have been known to slip a stick through their rivals' spokes to make them crash.

Races start when an official drops a handkerchief. There are four teams in each race, the blues, whites, reds, and greens. Each race lasts for seven 1 mile laps of the wall, or *spina*, in the middle of the arena.

The Circus is a very popular place for secret meetings between lovers.

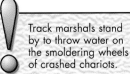
Track marshals stand by to throw water on the smoldering wheels of crashed chariots.

Look for the seven dolphins on the *spina*. One is removed to mark each lap.

Chariot racing is popular with all age groups. Children from wealthy families are given small chariots to play in that are pulled by donkeys or goats.

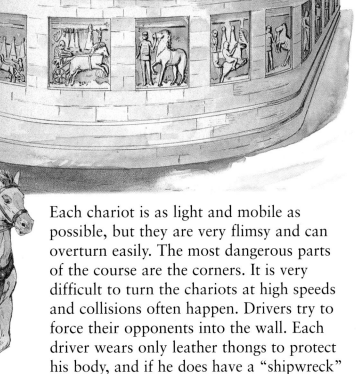

Each chariot is as light and mobile as possible, but they are very flimsy and can overturn easily. The most dangerous parts of the course are the corners. It is very difficult to turn the chariots at high speeds and collisions often happen. Drivers try to force their opponents into the wall. Each driver wears only leather thongs to protect his body, and if he does have a "shipwreck" he is likely to be badly injured or killed.

The Colosseum

No visitor to Rome should miss the impressive Flavian Amphitheater—also known as the Colosseum—which can be seen from all over the city. It is the biggest amphitheater in the world, and can hold 55,000 spectators. Try to visit on a public holiday, when everyone can get in free to watch the spectacular and bloodthirsty shows that take place there.

Exotic creatures from all over the known world are brought to Rome to appear at the Colosseum. The crowd's favorites are the ferocious lions, which are set loose on helpless criminals.

Gladiators are either slaves, prisoners, or criminals. If the crowd likes them, they may get gifts of coins, but only those who survive many fights will be set free. The lucky few are given bone tablets with their names on them to prove they are now free men.

Don't worry about the huge crowds at the Colosseum— there are 80 entrances, so you should be able to find a seat quickly. When you are inside, your head will be protected from the strong sun by an enormous canvas awning that can be moved back and forth by teams of slaves who pull on hundreds of ropes outside the arena.

To keep the people happy, there are over 100 public holidays in Rome every year.

Prisoners and wild beasts are kept in a maze of cages under the arena's floor.

Why not place a bet on your favorite gladiator? If he wins his fight, you'll be rich!

Gladiator fights are the most popular entertainment here. Many fighters come out into the arena together, and draw lots to see which men will fight each other to the death. There are several different types of gladiator, each with their own weapons, armor, strengths, and weaknesses.

Many people cheer for the brave and nimble *retarius*, who tries to snare his enemy in a net and then stab him with his trident. Others prefer the *secutor*, whose heavy equipment makes him slow but powerful.

Heavy helmets give gladiators protection, but they are difficult to see out of, which is risky when fighting a fast opponent.

Sightseers' tip

Keep an eye on the emperor—he decides whether a beaten gladiator should live or die. If he gives the thumbs up, the man will live—but if it is thumbs down, he will be killed by his opponent.

25

Around Rome

Although the city of Rome dominates this part of Italy, it is well worth taking a trip to the beautiful countryside beyond it. The way of life is slower here, but it is crucial to the well-being of the empire. Much of the land is covered by vast farm estates, owned by the wealthiest men in Rome, which supply much of the food that keeps the city going. Wine and olive oil are the most important crops. They are carried in huge quantities to giant ports on the Mediterranean coast and exported by sea all over the empire.

Sightseers' tip

Try to buy some fresh honey made from one of the estates' beehives. It is the only way to sweeten your food.

Just 16 miles from Rome at the mouth of the Tiber River, Ostia is the world's busiest port. The emperors have widened its harbor several times to handle the huge number of ships. Large warehouses on the seafront store grain, wine, and olive oil before barges take them up the Tiber to Rome.

Poor quality grapes are made into wine for workers to drink.

Farms are run by the manager, the *vilicus*. He is often a trusted slave.

The mild climate is good for crops, but the Italian soil is often poor.

Most rich families only visit the estates in the summer to get out of the sweltering city. But there is a workforce of slaves on the farms year-round to tend to the crops and livestock.

A nobleman's villa sits at the heart of each estate, surrounded by houses for slaves and farm workers, market gardens, and vineyards. In the fall, the grapes are picked and crushed by slaves to extract the juice. This is poured into large half-buried jars to ferment and become wine. The jars are sealed with pitch to keep out the rain.

When the olives are harvested from the trees, they are piled into an olive press. Slaves pull the handles down to press the olives and squeeze the oil out into jars.

All around Rome, gigantic aqueducts radiate out across the countryside to distant water sources. They supply over 40 million gallons of water to the city every day, mostly for baths and fountains. The water moves by gravity, so each aqueduct has to constantly angle downhill all along its length. At the top, stone slabs cover the water channel to keep out dirt.

Survival guide

R ome is a vibrant, cosmopolitan city filled with visitors from lands all over the empire. It has everything you need to enjoy your stay. However, it is also a place where laws are strictly enforced, and it is important not to fall foul of the authorities, who will punish noncitizens severely for any misdemeanor.

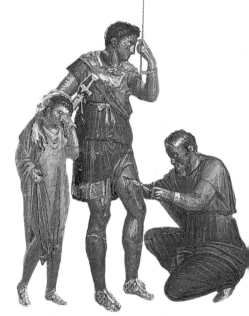

Magistrates are still officially elected to public posts by Rome's citizens. To win support, these rich men will spend a lot of money to please the people.

Society

Visitors must be aware of the rigidly defined levels of Roman society. At the top are Roman citizens, who are divided into the wealthy nobility and the ordinary people, or *plebeians*. Noncitizens from outside Rome have fewer rights. Below all these are the slaves, who do most of the work on farms and in the city. Slaves have almost no rights at all, but they can be freed by their master. Hadrian has just passed a law forbidding masters from killing slaves without a trial.

Administration

The emperor has absolute power. He appoints all the most important officials, who come from the rich nobility. Wealthy young men follow political careers, as lawyers, magistrates, and finally, as the governors of far-flung regions of the empire.

Surgeons have sophisticated tools to operate on wounds and broken bones, but the only painkillers available are poppy juice and wine.

Noncitizens and slaves who steal from temples are thrown to wild animals.

 To prevent uprisings, the Praetorian Guard is the only legion allowed near Rome.

 Romans are tolerant of different religions, but Christians are sometimes persecuted.

Four squads of special legionaries carry out police duties in Rome. In times of serious disturbance, the Praetorian Guard is called in.

Law and Order

Discipline is very important to the Romans, and you would be wise not to break their laws during your stay. Minor crimes are punished by beating. Thieves are branded. For the worst offenses, slaves can be executed by crucifixion. An elite force of legionaries, the Praetorian Guard, protects the body of the emperor himself.

Health

Medicine is based largely on herbal remedies and is not always very effective. For broken ribs, for example, the writer Pliny recommends applying a mix of goat's dung and wine to the wound.

Some slaves wear special tags with their master's name and address. If they run away, they can be caught and returned.

29

❓ Souvenir quiz

During your stay in Rome, you can see many amazing things. Before you leave, test your knowledge with this fun quiz. You will find the answers on page 32.

1. The Roman Forum is the most historic site in the city. How did it first start out?

a) As a hilltop fortress.

b) As a market place in a village.

c) As a temple to Romulus, founder of Rome.

2. What kind of creature raised Romulus and his brother?

a) A wolf.

b) A bear.

c) An eagle.

3. What will keep you awake if you rent a room near street level?

a) Traders' carts bringing goods into the city at night.

b) All-night chariot races through the streets.

c) Drunken revelers on their way home from wild parties.

4. What do fashionable Roman women make their wigs out of?

a) Horse hair from Arabian stallions.

b) Human hair from foreign slaves.

c) Finely spun silk from the Far East.

5. Why would a Roman woman want to have a pale face?

a) To prove she's of pure Roman blood.

b) It is considered to be a sign of great health.

c) To prove she is rich enough to stay indoors and not do any work.

6. Precious goods are brought to Rome from all over the known world. But what is Rome's most vital import?

a) Swords from Asia Minor.

b) Grain from Africa.

c) Tea cups from Britain.

7. What is *liquamen*?

a) A mix of rotting fish guts and salt used as a sauce.

b) A strong alcoholic drink made from cranberries.

c) A mix of boar droppings and wine used to treat bad chest injuries.

8. What equipment does the *retarius* gladiator carry?

a) A weighted net and a trident.

b) A short sword and a heavy rectangular shield.

c) A light javelin and a round shield.

9. The *lares* are very important to most Romans. But who are they?

a) Rome's special fire brigade.

b) The chief priests of Jupiter working at the Pantheon.

c) Household gods who watch over each family.

10. What are "shipwrecks" and where do people go to watch them?

a) Merchant ships running aground in the harbor at Ostia.

b) Rich men's sedan chairs colliding in the Roman Forum.

c) Chariots crashing at the Circus Maximus.

11. Romans love going to the theater. What kind of play do they most like to see?

a) Greek tragedies, with plenty of death and sorrow.

b) Fast-paced comedies, with a lot of farcical situations and silly jokes.

c) Political satires, filled with angry jokes about the emperor.

Index

Acknowledgments

The consultant
David Nightingale M.A. (Oxon) teaches Greek and Roman history at the University of Kent at Canterbury, in England.

Inklink Firenze illustrators
Simone Boni, Alessandro Rabatti, Lorenzo Pieri, Luigi Critone, Lucia Mattioli, Francisco Petracchi, Theo Caneschi, Federico Ferniani, Alain Bressan, Concetta D'Amato

Additional illustrations
Richard Berridge, Luigi Galante, Nicki Palin, Thomas Troyer

Picture Research Manager
Jane Lambert

Picture credits
b = bottom, c = center, l = left, r = right, t = top

p.4cl The Bridgeman Art Library, London/New York/Museo Archeologico Nazionale, Naples; p.6cl AKG London/Erich Lessing; p.9tr The British Museum; c Scala; p.11tr The Bridgeman Art Library, London/New York/Louvre, Paris, France; p.12c Ancient Art & Architecture; p.15br The British Museum; p.17tr Ancient Art & Architecture; p.19tl Ancient Art & Architecture; p.20bl C. M. Dixon/British Museum; p.23tl Giraudon/Louvre, Paris; p.25cr AKG London/Museum für Deutsche Geschichte, Berlin; p.27cr AKG London/Erich Lessing; p.28br Scala

Every effort has been made to trace the copyright holders of the photographs. The publishers apologize for any inconvenience caused.

Souvenir quiz answers

1 = b) 2 = a) 3 = a) 4 = b) 5 = c) 6 = b) 7 = a) 8 = a)
9 = c) 10 = c) 11 = b)

The setting for this Sightseers guide is A.D. 128.